# WHO IS KING?

Mary Jane Pearce
Lynn Blair

Bonker Books

for
Charlotte, Gracie, Amie, Megan, Georgie, Rudy,
Charlie, Tyler, Shannon and Sophia.

One sunny morning, Henry the hippo, Cracker the crocodile, Morris the monkey, Leo the lion and Toga the tiger all gathered near the river bank to discuss who was king.

"It is common knowledge," roared Leo the lion, "that my luxurious mane and loud roar make me king."

"My acute hearing and speed," laughed Henry the hippo,
"would make me a better king than all of you!"

"No." Morris laughed leaping around.
"I am king, for I am far more flexible than anyone else here."

"I've the longest snout and the sharpest teeth," Cracker the crocodile said,
"surely that makes me king of the jungle?"

"I can catch a moving mouse," said Toga, " Hunt like a warrior and snap you in two.
No one here is faster, not one of you."

Emily the elephant walked casually forward.
"If you want to resolve this why not challenge one another to a race?"

Swimming and climbing would be difficult to mark out fairly.
I think a race with starting blocks from, let's say, here to the tree
in the distance and back again?
Impressed with her suggestion the animals agreed.

Calling to the elephants Emily had them roll some logs into five starting positions.
At the very back was Henry the hippo, then Leo the lion, Toga the tiger,
Morris the monkey, then Cracker the crocodile.
Sounding her trunk Emily gave them the go ahead.

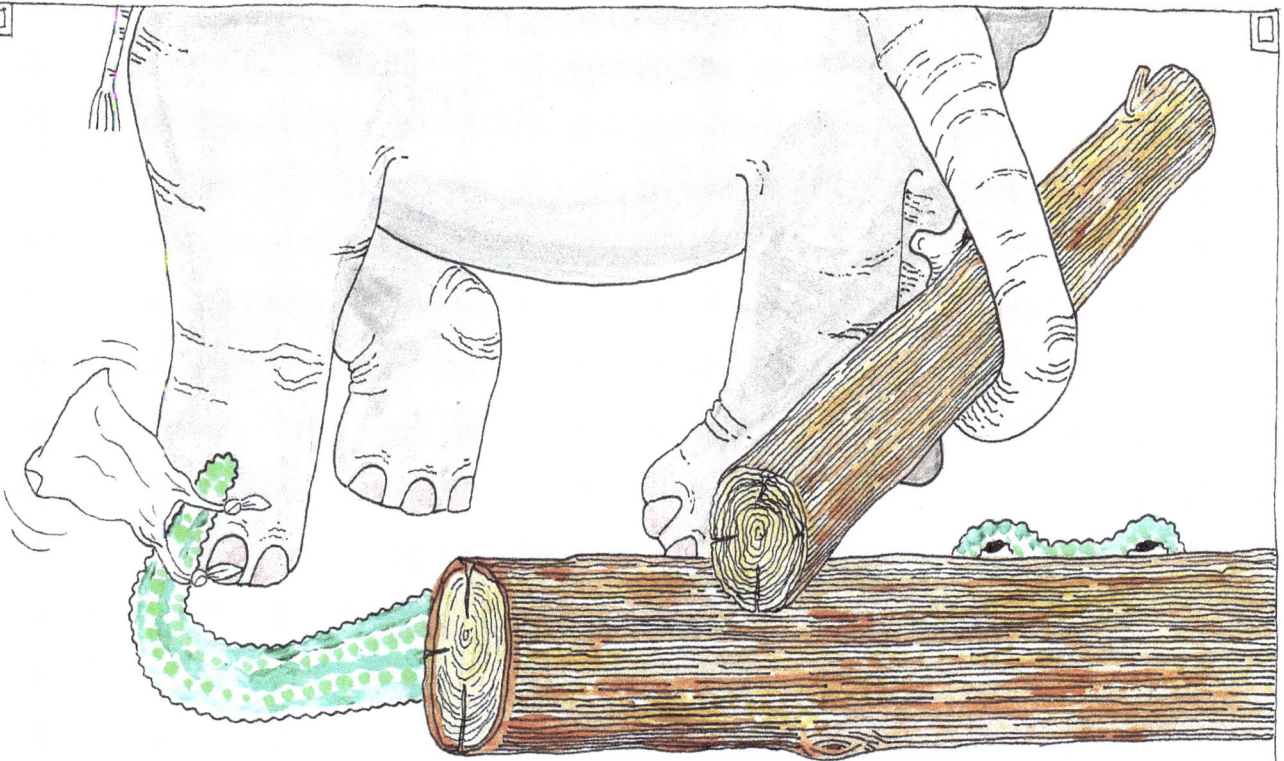

Running like the wind Henry hippo left a trail of dust behind.
Not far behind him was Leo the lion.
Morris was disappointed to discover that his legs were nowhere near as nimble as his arms.
Toga the tiger was seen overtaking Leo Lion.
Disappearing into the dust that Henry had kicked up they
were soon all out of sight.

Spinning around the tree they were quickly on their way back.
First to finish the race was Toga the tiger, second was Henry hippo,
then Leo, then Cracker, then Morris. They had barely caught their breath
when they began arguing again.

"You are all kings!" Emily and the elephants roared.
"How is that so?" Leo asked.
"Well," Emily began, "It's true tiger won this race, but, for example,
he wouldn't be able to climb trees as fast as Morris."

The animals all stared at one another, turning to Emily they said.
"Then you must be a queen because of your long trunk?"
"That is right, we are all individuals. Wouldn't life be boring if we were all the same in looks and skills?"

Nodding in agreement the animals felt content.
Morris headed back to the trees. Cracker went back into the water.
Toga disappeared into the jungle. Henry the hippo sunk into the mud
and Leo the lion returned to his sun spot.

The moral of this story is...

"Though we are all different, we are all capable of so much."

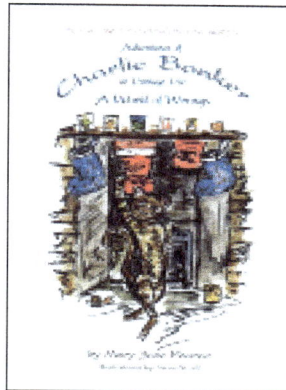

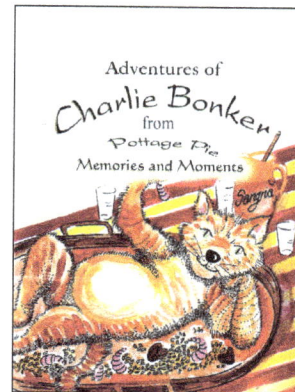

Meet Charlie and his friends and follow them through their wild adventures.

www.bonkerbooks.com

# Millie the Mole
## and the Unfamiliar Hole

by M J Pearce

Illustrations by Hulya Harber

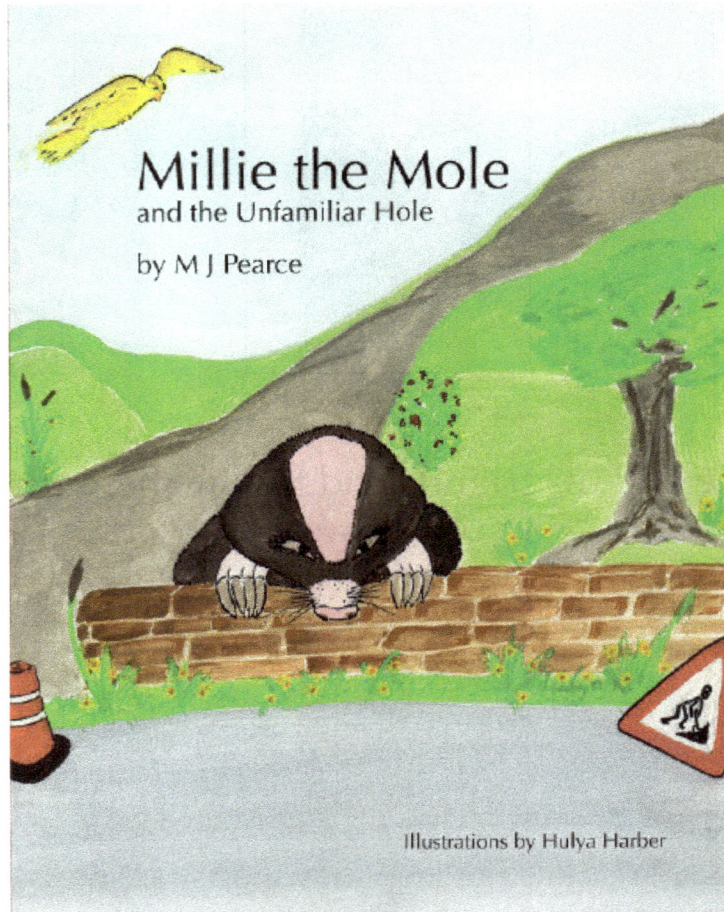

www.bonkerbooks.com

www.ingramcontent.com/pod-product-compliance
Lightning Source LLC
Chambersburg PA
CBHW081453070426
42452CB00042B/2718